VICTORIAN LIFE

A VICTORIAN STREET

RICHARD WOOD

Wayland

VICTORIAN LIFE

A VICTORIAN CHRISTMAS

A VICTORIAN FACTORY

A VICTORIAN HOLIDAY

A VICTORIAN SCHOOL

A VICTORIAN STREET

A VICTORIAN SUNDAY

VICTORIAN CLOTHES

VICTORIAN TRANSPORT

HOW WE LEARN ABOUT THE VICTORIANS

Queen Victoria reigned from 1837 to 1901, a time when Britain went through enormous social and industrial changes. We can learn about Victorians in various ways. We can still see many of their buildings standing today, we can look at their documents, maps and artefacts – many of which can be found in museums. Photography, invented during Victoria's reign, gives us a good picture of life in Victorian Britain. In this book you will see what Victorian life was like through some of this historical evidence.

Series design: Pardoe Blacker Ltd
Editor: Sarah Doughty

First published in 1993 by Wayland (Publishers) Ltd,
61 Western Road, Hove, East Sussex BN3 1JD, England

© Copyright 1993 Wayland (Publishers) Ltd

British Library Cataloguing in Publication Data
Wood, Richard
  Victorian Street. - (Victorian Life Series)
  I. Title II. Series
  941.081

ISBN 0 7502 0793 0

Printed and bound in Great Britain by B.P.C.C
Paulton Books

Cover picture: A busy Victorian street in London.

Picture acknowledgements
E.T Archive *cover*, 4, 12, 20, 21 (bottom), 23 (both); Mary Evans 5 (top), 6 (Bruce Castle Museum), 7 (top), 8, 9 (both), 10, 11 (left), 13 (top), 14, 15 (bottom), 16, 17, 18 (both), 19 (bottom), 21 (top), 24, 26 (bottom), 27; Hulton Picture Library 7 (bottom), 19 (top), 25 (bottom); Mansell Collection 25 (top); Sefton 13 (bottom); Salvation Army 26 (top); Tate Gallery, London 22; Richard Wood 5 (bottom), 11 (right). The artwork on page 15 is by Annabel Spenceley.

CONTENTS

4

ON THE STREET

8

STREET SERVICES

12

BUILDINGS ON THE STREET

16

STREET RESIDENTS

20

THE STREET AT WORK

24

STREET LIFE

28 TIMELINE

30 GLOSSARY

31 BOOKS TO READ

32 INDEX

ON THE STREET

Do you enjoy walking down a busy street? There is usually something interesting to see. There are shop windows to look in, people to meet and traffic to watch out for. Streets can be places to live, places to work, places of entertainment or just places to pass the time with friends. Victorian streets were like this too. But the sights, sounds and smells were often different from today.

A LONDON STREET

See how many differences you can spot between this view of a London street in 1825 on the right, and a modern town-centre street. Notice the jumble of different types of buildings in the Victorian street, most of which have tall chimneys for coal fires. The surface of the road looks very rough. It must have been quiet with so little traffic. But the street is busy with people, selling things or buying from the many small shops.

The Strand, London, 1825.

A VILLAGE STREET

Village streets, like the one in the picture on the right, were quieter still. The road made a good place for children to play. Neighbours often met for a chat at the front door or over the garden gate. But poor people were not supposed to speak to 'their betters' (richer people) unless they were spoken to first. How can you tell what 'class' the people in the picture belong to?

Chatting at the gate, about 1875.

STREET NAMES

Many towns grew very rapidly during the nineteenth century. People could not find their way round all the new streets of similar houses. So iron name plates were put at street corners, and houses were given numbers to help the postmen find where people lived. *Victoria Road* was a popular new street name in many towns.

The name plate for Victoria Road, Maldon.

·VICTORIA·ROAD

HORSE BUS

As towns got bigger, people had to live further out from the centre. Sometimes they travelled long distances to work or to visit shops or friends. Only very rich people owned their own horses and carriages. Better-off people hired horse-drawn taxis called hansom cabs, but most people travelled by horse-drawn omnibus. These were first introduced in 1829 and carried twelve people inside and ten people on top. The driver sat outside in all weathers. Like modern buses, the sides were covered with advertisements for groceries and household goods.

London horse bus, about 1900.

CROSSING SWEEPER

Victorian streets were filthy. They were covered with the droppings of many horses as well as rubbish that was often thrown into open drains in the road. The iron wheels of carts, carriages and buses broke up the stone surface into tiny pieces. In summer, streets were sprayed with water to keep down the dust. In winter, they were often covered in deep mud. Better-off people paid a crossing sweeper, like the man on the right, to clear a path for them to cross the road.

The crossing sweeper, about 1900.

MOTOR CARS

By the 1890s, rich people could buy petrol-powered cars for pleasure motoring. But some people were scared of these new 'monsters' on the streets. The law said that a man must walk in front of every car, holding a red flag as a warning. In 1896, the red flag rule was dropped and the speed limit raised from 10 mph to 14 mph. The streets of Britain would never be as quiet again.

Victorian motor cars.

Nearly everybody in Britain today has mains water, drains, electricity and perhaps gas. Post is delivered to our doors regularly. If we are in trouble, we can telephone for help from doctors, police or fire services. Most people in the past were not so lucky. In Victorian times, services like these only slowly became available to more people.

STREET LIGHTING

Dark streets are often dangerous. The invention of gas lighting in 1791 made bright street lights possible. In the 1830s, more and more towns put up gas street lamps. Each lamp was lit separately every evening by a lamplighter. Next morning he turned them all off again. Sometimes people paid him to wake them up by tapping on their bedroom windows with his long pole. Gas lights were brighter and cleaner than candles or oil lamps. From the 1880s, electric street lights began to replace gas ones in large towns.

The lamplighter, 1840s.

WATER PUMP

In Britain today we have taps in our homes and a constant supply of clean water. In Victorian times, most people fetched water from rivers, wells or street pumps like this one. Carrying water in jugs and buckets was a heavy job, especially for children. Clean water was precious so they were very careful not to waste the water by spilling it.

The village pump.

THE SPREAD OF DISEASE

Victorian streets could be unhealthy places to live. Too many people were crowded together without proper drains or pure water. Diseases like cholera and typhoid spread rapidly in these conditions, so warnings like the one on this poster were put up for everyone to see. Until the 1880s, many towns had regular cholera epidemics which killed thousands of people.

BOARD OF WORKS
FOR THE LIMEHOUSE DISTRICT.
COMPRISING LIMEHOUSE, RATCLIFF, SHADWELL & WAPPING.

In consequence of the appearance of **CHOLERA** within this District, the Board have appointed the under-mentioned Medical Gentlemen who will give ADVICE, MEDICINE, AND ASSISTANCE, FREE OF ANY CHARGE, AND UPON APPLICATION, AT ANY HOUR OF THE DAY OR NIGHT.

The Inhabitants are earnestly requested not to neglect the first symptoms of the appearance of Disease, (which in its early stage is easy to cure), but to apply, WITHOUT DELAY, to one of the Medical Gentlemen appointed.

The Board have opened an Establishment for the reception of Patients, in a building at Green Bank, near Wapping Church, (formerly used as Wapping Workhouse), where all cases of Cholera and Diarrhœa will be received and placed under the care of a competent Resident Medical Practitioner, and proper Attendants.

THE FOLLOWING ARE THE MEDICAL GENTLEMEN TO BE APPLIED TO:--
Mr. ORTON,
56, White Horse Street.
Dr. NIGHTINGALL,
4, Commercial Terrace, Commercial Road, (near Limehouse Church.)
Mr. SCHROEDER,
53, Three Colt Street, Limehouse.
Mr. HARRIS,
5, York Terrace, Commercial Road, (opposite Stepney Railway Station.)
Mr. CAMBELL,
At Mr. GRAY's, Chemist, Old Road, opposite "The World's End."
Mr. LYNCH,
St. James's Terrace, Back Road, Shadwell.
Mr. HECKFORD,
At the Dispensary, Wapping Workhouse.

BOARD OFFICES, WHITE HORSE STREET, 26th July, 1866.
BY ORDER,
THOS. W. RATCLIFF,
Clerk to the Board.

Cholera warning, 1866.

DIRTY DRAINS

Look carefully along your street, and you may find the covers of the drains which run underneath. These sewers may have been built in Victorian times. Most people thought that disease was carried in the air. But in 1853, during a cholera epidemic, a doctor, John Snow, proved that the illness was spread by dirty water. Wells were made dirty by sewage from nearby cesspits. River water was even worse. Drains emptying into rivers often made them stink with filth.

In 1865, London became one of the first cities to build proper sewers. Pipes were also laid on to supply pure water direct to people's homes. Streets were at last becoming cleaner and healthier places to live.

Inspecting the sewers, 1890.

FIRE BRIGADE

Fire was another serious risk. Most people used open fires for heating and cooking. After dark they lit candles and oil or gas lamps. Fire could spread rapidly where houses were tightly packed together. From the 1860s, many towns bought steam-powered fire-engines like the one shown on the opposite page.

Horses pulled the engine to the scene of the fire. There it was connected to a well or water pipe under the road. The steam pumps sprayed the burning building with water. They were much more efficient than the buckets or hand pumps that had been available before.

Southampton fire brigade, 1885.

Victorian post-box in Norwich.

THE PENNY POST

Keeping in touch with family and friends in other places was not always easy. But in 1840, the Penny Post was started by Rowland Hill. Stamps were sold showing Queen Victoria's head. At first letters had to be taken to post offices. But from 1852, cast iron post-boxes were put on the streets. These were coloured green until 1874 when they were all painted bright red.

Some Victorian post-boxes, like this one, are still in use. Look for the letters VR, which stands for *Victoria Regina*, on the front.

BUILDINGS ON THE STREET

Victorian streets often had many different types of buildings. Old ones were modernized in Victorian style. But it was a busy time for new building too. Was your house or school built in Victorian times? Look for dates on walls which tell how old buildings are. Most Victorian buildings are strong and have lasted well.

THE BUSY HIGH STREET

This picture shows a busy main street at the end of the century. Compare it with the picture of the street in 1825 on page 4. You will see that it looks much busier. The lampposts, telephone wires, large shop windows and advertisements make it much more like a modern street scene. By the end of the century, few people lived in the town centre. Most had moved out to suburbs on the edge of the town. Village streets were different. They still had a mixture of houses and other types of buildings.

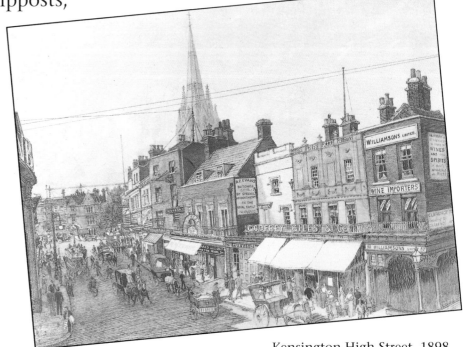

Kensington High Street, 1898.

HOMES FOR POOR PEOPLE

There was always a shortage of houses, particularly for the poorest people. Sometimes several families shared one small house, like the houses at the back of this picture below.

In the big cities, like London, Glasgow and Edinburgh, new blocks of flats were built. They may have looked a bit like prisons, but poor families were glad to have homes of their own.

New housing for the poor, 1879.

PUBLIC BUILDINGS

Public buildings like churches, stations and town halls like this one to the right, were often built on a very grand scale. Towns competed with each other to have the biggest and best. These new buildings were often decorated with different coloured bricks, imitation stonework or even statues. Railway transport made it cheaper for builders to buy different materials and ready-made decorations.

Manchester Town Hall.

VICTORIAN TERRACED HOUSES

New homes were often built in long terraces of identical houses with shops at street corners. These were cheap to build because their side walls were shared. The poorest were built 'back to back'. In some of these, even back walls were shared, so there was no space for a yard. Most have now been pulled down as they are no longer thought fit to live in.

Better-quality terraces had front and back gardens and were strongly built. Victorian builders bought land on the edge of towns and built whole streets of terraced houses.

As each one was completed it was sold or rented from a landlord.

Houses like the one on the opposite page were very common. You may know of some near you. This shows a house has a hall entrance, a back extension containing a scullery (for cleaning and washing) and a flush toilet. There is a front parlour (only used on special occasions) and three bedrooms but no bathroom. Houses like this cost £150 to build. Cheaper types had just two rooms on each floor with the front door opening into the living room.

Victorian slums.

Front

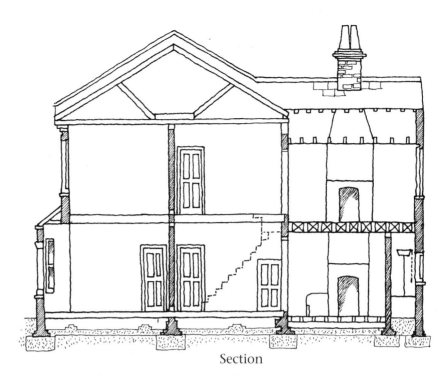

Section

Diagrams showing a terraced house from the front and side.

STREET FURNITURE

Until Victorian times, builders only used materials that were made or found locally. Every part of Britain had a different style of buildings. But from the 1850s, a wide range of new items could be ordered from catalogues and delivered by train. Slates from Wales, yellow bricks from East Anglia and door mouldings from factories in the Midlands could now be seen anywhere in Britain. This picture shows some of the cast iron items from northern iron works that became common on Victorian streets.

Cast iron street fittings.

STREET RESIDENTS

Big towns were often divided into areas lived in by different sorts of people. There were wide, leafy streets of detached houses for well-off middle-class people. Other areas had narrow streets of small houses with tiny yards and not a tree in sight. This is where poor factory workers lived. Country towns and villages were usually more mixed.

LIVING IN THE COUNTRYSIDE

Life in the countryside was quieter and cleaner than town life. Some people never left the village they were born in. They married people from the same street and knew their neighbours as well as they knew their own families. Life for poor country people was hard. Wages were so low that many men moved to towns to find better-paid work. Country cottages were small and dark. Street services like sewers, piped water and gas were not available.

The village street, about 1875.

A TOWN FAMILY

This London family below are shown arriving home from church. In this middle-class family, 'papa' probably worked in a city office, to which he would travel by train or cab. 'Mama' spent her time reading, sewing or paying calls to friends. The housework was done for her by maids. She may have sometimes been bored and wished she had more freedom. The children would attend private schools to avoid mixing with 'common' children. Many of their friends came from much larger families. But at least their house was big enough for them all to have bedrooms of their own.

Middle-class family returning home, 1855.

MIDDLE-CLASS SUBURBS

There were many houses like this in middle-class suburbs on the edge of towns. They gave well-off families spacious rooms, large gardens and privacy from the street. A separate tradesman's entrance round the back hid delivery men and servants from view. Can you see the attic windows? Two or three live-in maids might have slept up there.

A detached villa of the 1890s.

A maid cleaning steps, 1870s.

MAID OF ALL WORK

This was a common sight in middle-class areas. Most families earning over £3 a week employed a young 'maid of all work'. She did the family's cleaning, cooking, washing and mending and nursed the children. She worked from 6 am to 10 pm with half a day off every week. It was often a lonely life. Well-off families sometimes had several servants including a cook and nanny. Only very rich people could afford the luxury of men servants such as a butler or footman.

POOR FAMILIES

Life for the poor was a constant struggle. Home was often a single room. Several children shared the bed, covering themselves with rags to keep warm. Their food was mainly bread and potatoes. When their parents were out of work the whole family often went hungry. Perhaps the girl in the picture worked 'in service' with a middle-class family, and the few shillings a week she earned helped to keep her family from starving.

A poor family in London's East End, 1900s.

NARROW ALLEYWAYS

In some old streets you can still find dark alleys (called wynds in Scotland) between the houses. In Victorian times these led to the courts of tiny, damp houses where the poorest people lived. They had no clean water or drains. Even the air they breathed was full of smoke from surrounding chimneys. A report on living conditions in 1842 found that 57 per cent of poor children in Manchester died before they were 5 years old. Conditions improved, but slowly. For many people the 'good old days' were not good at all!

A narrow wynd in Edinburgh, about 1840.

THE STREET AT WORK

Do many people earn their living on your street? Some may work at home. Others work in shops and offices, schools or factories, or on the street itself. Victorian streets were like this too. They were often full of people working hard to earn enough to support their families.

THE BUTCHER'S SHOP

Most Victorian shops were small. Their owners often lived over the shop. Can you see the butcher with his knife in this picture? His son on the right is holding a customer's pony and trap. There were no supermarkets in Victorian times. Most groceries were sold loose – they were cut up and weighed for each customer. Better-off people usually had their shopping delivered in carts like the baker's cart on the left of the picture.

A Surrey butcher's shop, about 1900.

THE BLACKSMITH

In early Victorian times, iron items were often handmade by local blacksmiths. Later on, most things were mass produced in factories. Rail transport made it possible to buy goods cheaply from every part of Britain or even abroad. Skilled smiths and farriers were still needed. They made shoes and harnesses for all the horses working in the streets and on farms. Nearly every village had a 'smithy' like this one.

The blacksmith's shop.

Shoe black at work, 1892.

WORKING IN THE STREET

This man set up shop on the pavement and cleaned shoes for a living. Other people worked at home. They made things like shirts, shoes, straw hats and lace cloths for shops and factories. Many young children also worked at home. But in 1874, a new law made it illegal for young children to work full time. After 1880, all children under 10 had to attend school.

THE MARKET PLACE

The street really came alive on market day!
Brightly-coloured stalls were set up and the
streets were full of shoppers hunting for
bargains. Country people brought their carts
loaded with fresh vegetables, eggs and cheese,
live rabbits and hens. Fishermen sold oysters
and mussels, sea fish or eels still wriggling in
bowls of water. Travelling tradesmen sold
fabrics, books, china and glass. Each shouted
out that his wares were the best in town. Often
the streets were full of animals too. Sheep and
cows, pigs and poultry were herded along the
roads to the livestock market.

Norwich Market Place, 1830s.

STREET SELLERS

This man on the left probably looked much older than he was. His hat and coat were someone else's cast-offs and did not fit him well. His trousers were patched and his shoes full of holes. He had no socks. Perhaps kind people took pity on him and bought his matches to help him. There were 30,000 men, women and children like him selling things on the streets of London in 1851. It was a very hard way to earn a living.

Match seller, 1892.

Just like today, Victorian people could often buy hot food on the street. Many poor people had no ovens, so anything baked was a treat. This man's oven is mounted on a cart. He wheeled it from street to street selling hot potatoes for 1d (½p) each. They made a filling lunch during a break from work.

The baked potato seller, 1892.

STREET
LIFE

Is your favourite street a lively place? Victorian streets were often busy, noisy and full of activity all day long. The street was still a safe place for children to play, and there was usually plenty of entertainment for them to enjoy.

The organ grinder, 1886.

STREET ENTERTAINMENT

These children stopped on their way home from school to listen to the organ grinder. The organ was slung from his neck. When he turned the handle on the side, it played well-known tunes. The organ grinder's pet monkey danced in time with the music. Then it held out a hat to beg from passers-by who had stopped to watch. Today, buskers still occasionally play music in the street. But we would be very surprised to see a monkey!

THE MUFFIN MAN

Every day the muffin man brought freshly-baked muffins for breakfast or tea. He carried them in a tray on his head, covered with a cloth to keep them warm. People listened out for his bell and his call of 'muffins, fresh muffins'.

All the street traders had different cries. Children imitated them, calling 'ropes of onions, ropes of onions', 'rags and bones','buy a dish of eels','oranges fresh and fair','sweep, sweep, chimney sweep', or 'knives to grind'. They especially liked to watch the shower of sparks from the knife-grinder's wheel.

The muffin man, about 1900.

PUBLIC HOUSES

In some towns, almost every street had at least one public house. On sunny days people sat outside on benches and drank frothy beer from pint mugs. Most of the customers were men. They met their friends here after work to drink, play cards or perhaps have a game of skittles or bowls.

Outside the ale house, 1877.

THE PIE SHOP

This shop sold hot eel or meat pies for 1d (½p) or 2d (1p). For these children, even this seemed a lot of money. Some days they went hungry, or had to beg for food. During Queen Victoria's reign, conditions for the poorest people slowly improved. But even at the end of her reign, some children still walked the streets in bare feet and dressed in rags. A survey of York in 1899 found that a quarter of all families lived in poverty.

Poor children outside the pie shop, about 1900.

STREET CRIME

Perhaps this little boy stole some food or tried to pick someone's pocket. Street crime was a serious problem in the early nineteenth century. Some hungry people were forced to steal to keep their families from starving. Others took advantage of dimly-lit streets to help themselves to other people's property.

Britain's first paid police force was set up in London by Sir Robert Peel in 1829. 'Bobbies' or 'peelers' wore blue coats and hard top hats and were soon a common sight on the streets.

London police arrest a thief, 1869.

Crime rates fell. Soon other towns started police forces of their own. In 1856, the Police Act said that all areas should have paid police. By 1901, there were 45,000 policemen on the streets of Britain.

The Queen's Diamond Jubilee procession, 1897.

STREET PARTIES

In 1897, Queen Victoria had been on the throne for sixty years. Britain was then the richest country in the world. Most people's lives were more comfortable than ever before. The streets were cleaner and safer, and fewer people died of preventable diseases. To celebrate the sixtieth year of Victoria's reign, street parties were organized. Flags flew, bands played, food was served and drink flowed. All over the country, millions of people lined the streets and cheered, 'God save the Queen'.

TIME LINE

EARLY 1800s

1825 First railway built by George Stephenson from Stockton to Darlington.

1829 Sir Robert Peel's Police Act sets up a police force in London. Horse-drawn bus service begins.

1830s

1831 Population of Britain is 16 million.

1833 Lord Shaftesbury's Factory Act forbids children under 18 to work more than 12 hours per day.

1834 Hansom cab invented by Joseph Hansom. Serious cholera epidemic.

1837 Queen Victoria's reign begins.

1839 First bicycle invented by Kirkpatrick MacMillan of Dumfries, Scotland. Photography invented by Louis Daguerre of Paris.

1840s

1840 Lord Shaftesbury's Act forbids children to be chimney sweeps.

1845 Health of Towns Commission reports on the living conditions of the poor. Pottery drainpipes invented.

1848 Electric lights first demonstrated in London. Serious cholera epidemic.

1849 Public Health Acts aim to improve conditions.

1850s

1851 Many new inventions on show at The Great Exhibition.

1852 Post-boxes first placed on streets.

1853 During a cholera epidemic, Dr Snow discovers that the disease is carried in polluted drinking water.

1856 Police Act says all counties must set up police forces.

1858 First trams operate in Birkenhead. 'The Great Stink' in London caused by sewers emptying into the River Thames.

1860s

1861 Mrs. Beeton's 'Book of Household Management' published.

1863 Competition for steam fire-engines held at Crystal Palace.

1865 First efficient sewer system opened in London. Salvation Army founded by 'General' William Booth to bring religion and help to the poor.

1867 Dr Thomas Barnardo opens his first home for homeless orphans.

1868 Hanging of criminals in public is ended.

1870s

1870 Rubber tyres first used. Telephone invented by Alexander Graham Bell.

1874 Factory Act forbids children to work more than 10 hours per day. Post-boxes on streets painted bright red.

1875 Artisan's Dwelling Act allows clearance of slum houses to build new homes for the poor.

1877 Society for the Protection of Ancient Buildings founded.

1879 First London streets lit by electricity.

1880s

1880 Education Act makes school compulsory for all children to the age of 10. Penny farthing bicycle invented.

1885 First motor car built by Daimler Benz.

1886 Safety bicycles first made by the Rover Company.

1889 Pneumatic (inflated) rubber tyres invented by John Dunlop of Belfast.

1890s

1896 Motor cars allowed to travel at up to 14 mph without red flag.

1897 Queen Victoria's Diamond Jubilee celebrated throughout the British Empire.

1899 Seebohm Rowntree's survey of York finds a quarter of the population living in poverty.

1900s

1901 Population of Britain now 37 million. Coal tar first used to make smooth road surfaces. Death of Queen Victoria.

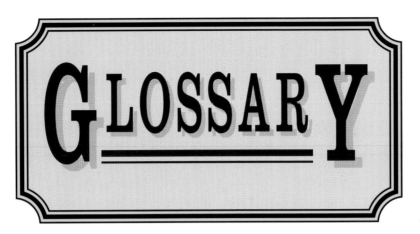

GLOSSARY

Act (of Parliament) When a new law is made.

Attic A room at the top of the house, under the roof.

Blacksmith Someone who makes things out of iron.

Busker Someone who plays music on the street.

Catalogue A list of things for sale.

Cesspit A hole in the ground for collecting filthy waste.

Cholera A dangerous disease usually caused by drinking dirty water.

Contamination When something has been made dirty or infected.

Court An area enclosed by walls or buildings.

Detached house A house that stands on its own.

Epidemic A serious and widespread outbreak of disease.

Farrier Someone who shoes horses.

Grind To sharpen on a stone.

Hansom cab A two-seated taxi pulled by one horse.

Identical Exactly the same.

Jubilee A special anniversary.

Livestock Farm animals.

Mouldings Decorated building materials made in moulds.

Omnibus A Victorian word for bus.

Parlour The smartest or best sitting room.

Preventable Something that could have been avoided.

Regina The Latin word for queen.

Scullery A room for rough kitchen work and cleaning.

Sewage Filthy waste from toilets and drains.

Sewers Underground pipes or tunnels for removing waste matter.

Slums Poor houses that are unfit for people to live in.

Suburbs Districts on the edge of towns and cities.

Terraces Rows of houses all joined together.

Trap A small carriage pulled by one horse or pony.

Typhoid fever A dangerous infection causing red spots on the skin.

Wynd A Scottish word for a narrow lane or alley.

BOOKS TO READ

Conner, E. *A Child in Victorian London* (Wayland, 1986)

Dunning, R. *Victorian Life and Transport* (Nelson, 1981)

Evans, A. *Finding out about Victorian Law and Order* (Batsford, 1988)

Rawcliffe, M. *Finding out about Victorian London* (Batsford, 1985)

Rawcliffe, M. *Finding out about Victorian Public Health and Housing* (Batsford, 1987)

Sauvain, P. *A Victorian Factory Town* (Macmillan, 1979)

Seaman, L. *Life in Victorian London* (Batsford 1973)

Tanner, Q. *Rubbish* (A & C Black, 1991)

PLACES TO VISIT

Many museums and historic houses have displays about Victorian life. Find out what your local museums contain. Here is a selection.

ENGLAND

Berkshire: Museum of English Rural Life, Reading, RG6 2AG. Tel. 0734 318660

Birmingham: Museum of Science and Industry, Newhall Street, Birmingham, B3 1RZ. Tel. 021 236 1022

Cambridgeshire: City Museum and Art Gallery, Priestgate, Peterborough, PE1 1LF. Tel. 0733 43329

Cleveland: Preston Hall Museum, Yarm Road, Stockton-on-Tees, TS18 3RH. Tel. 0642 781184

Dorset: Waterfront Museum, Oakley's Mill, Paradise Street, The Quay, Poole, BH15 1HJ. Tel. 0202 683138

Durham: The North of England Open Air Museum, Beamish, County Durham, DH9 0RG. Tel. 0207 231811

Lincolnshire: Museum of Lincolnshire Life, The Old Barracks, Burton Road, Lincoln, LN1 3LY. Tel. 0522 528448

London: London Transport Museum, Covent Garden, London, WC2E 7BB. Tel. 071 3796344
Museum of London, London Wall, London, EC2Y 5HN. Tel. 071 6003699

Manchester: Museum of Science and Industry, Liverpool Road Station, Castlefield, Manchester, M3 4JP. Tel. 061 832 2244

Norfolk: Bridewell Museum of Trades and Industries, Bridewell Alley, Norwich, NR2 1AQ. Tel. 0603 667228

Nottinghamshire: Industrial Museum, Courtyard Buildings, Wollaton Park, Nottingham, NG8 2AE. Tel. 0602 284602

Shropshire: Ironbridge Gorge Museum, Ironbridge, Telford, TF8 7AW. Tel. 095245 3522

West Midlands: The Black Country Museum, Tipton Road, Dudley, DY1 4SQ. Tel. 021 5579643

Yorkshire and Humberside: Street Life: Hull Museum of Transport, High Street, Hull, HU1 3DX. Tel. 0482 222737

York Castle Museum, YO1 1RY. Tel. 0904 653611

SCOTLAND

Edinburgh: Huntly House Museum, 142 Canongate, Edinburgh, EH8 8DD. Tel. 031 225 2424 ext 6689
National Museums of Scotland, Chambers Street, Edinburgh, EH1 1JF, Tel. 031 2257534

Glasgow: Museum of Transport, Kelvin Hall, 1 Bunhouse Road, Glasgow, G3 8PZ, Tel. 041 3573929
Tenement House, 145 Buccleuch Street, Glasgow, G3 6QN. Tel. 041 3330183

WALES

Cardiff: Welsh Folk Museum, St. Fagans, Cardiff, CF5 6XB. Tel. 0222 569441

Welsh Industrial and Maritime Museum, Bute Street, Cardiff, CF1 6AN.

Swansea: Swansea Maritime and Industrial Museum, Museum Square, Maritime Quarter, Swansea, SA1 1SN. Tel. 0792 650351

NORTHERN IRELAND

Belfast: Ulster Folk and Transport Museum, Witham Street Gallery, Belfast, BT4 1HP. Tel. 0232 451519

INDEX

bicycle 28, 29
blacksmith 21
buskers 24

countryside 16
crime 26-7
crossing sweeper 7

Diamond Jubilee 27, 28
disease 9
drains 10

entertainment 24

fire brigade 10-11, 29

Great Exhibition 28

hansom cabs 6
high street 12
Hill, Rowland 11
horse-bus 6, 28

lampposts 12

maids 17, 18
market place 22
motor car 7, 29
muffin man 25

nanny 18
neighbours 5

Peel, Sir Robert 26, 28
Penny Post 11
photography 28
pie shop 26
post 8
post-boxes 11, 28, 29
public buildings 13
public houses 25

railways 13, 28

school 17, 21
Scotland 19
servants 18
sewers 10, 16, 28, 29
shops 4, 20
Snow, Dr John 10, 28
Stephenson, G. 28
street
   furniture 15
   lighting 8
   parties 27
   sellers 23
   services 8
suburbs 18

telephone 29
terraced houses 14-15

village 5

water pump 9

I.